Christina Meiser

A DOLLY NAMED MOLLY

WINTERS

A Dolly Named Molly
Copyright © 2018 by Christina Meiser. All rights reserved.

No part of this publication may be reproduced, stored in a retrieval system or transmitted in any way by any means, electronic, mechanical, photocopy, recording or otherwise without the prior permission of the author except as provided by USA copyright law.

The opinions expressed by the author are not necessarily those of Winters Publishing, LLC.

Published by Winters Publishing, LLC
2448 E. 81st St. Suite #4802 | Tulsa, Oklahoma 74137 USA

Book design copyright © 2014 by Winters Publishing, LLC. All rights reserved.

Published in the United States of America

ISBN: 9781947426016(paperback) 9781947426023(ebook)
1. Juvenile Fiction / Toys, Dolls & Puppets
2. Juvenile Fiction / Social Themes / Friendship

This book belongs to:

_____

As the lights turned off for the night, the store owner called out to the toys, "Don't worry my little friends, tomorrow is a new day. And there is a perfect home for each of you." With that, he closed the door.

A dolly named Molly let out a long sigh and sank down to the bottom of her box.

"There were so many children in the toy store today," she thought. "And yet I still don't have a home."

Molly was a ballerina and wore a beautiful gown, slippers, and crown. She longed to dance, play tea party and sleep alongside her new special friend.

As Molly began to cry, Mrs. Chestnut, the wisest of the stuffed animals crawled onto the shelf next to her and whispered, "Molly, please don't cry. You heard the store owner, there is a perfect home for all o us. Why don't we walk to the front window and dream about our new homes."

The sun was nearly gone, and Molly and Mrs. Chestnut watched as people rushed passed the window. Molly tried to imagine where each of them lived and what it was like.

The next day when the store owner opened the door, Molly and Mrs. Chestnut had to sneak back to their aisle so they would not be seen.

"Maybe today I would have a home," Molly thought, as she climed back into her box. She smoothed her hair, straightened her dress and smiled her brightest smile.

"Keep your head up darling. Today could be your day," said Mrs. Chestnut.

As the afternoon turned into evening, Molly watched sadly as children raced through the store, choosing fire trucks, race cars, robots, bicycles and even other dolls. It wasn't until a liggle girl scooped up Mrs. Chestnut into her arms, squealed with delight and ran off with her only friend that Molly felt lonelier than ever.

Molly waved good-bye as Mrs. Chestnut peered over the little girl's shoulder and said, "Molly, don't you worry. Your perfect home is waiting for you! You will dance with someone very soon!"

With that, Mrs. Chestnut was gone and Molly could see through the window that it was almost closing time.

Before the store owner left for the night, the door flew open causing the bells on the door to ring loudly. A man rushed into the store. All the toys stiffened and winced as he paced up and down the aisles.

"I have to get the perect gift," the man mumbled to himself.

Finally the store owner came to assist the man. "Can I help you? he asked.

"Yes, I have to get the perfect gift for my daughter and I don't have much time. She has been in the hospital, but she is coming home today and I want to surprise her with something perfect."

"Let me think," said the store owner.

Molly stood frozen in her box. This was not at all how she imagined being chosen from the store. Molly closed her eyes as the store owner and the man approached.

"My daughter loves ballet and this doll is wearing a dress." said the man. "I was hoping for something more cheerful and this doll looks a little sad."

"All the toys look a little sad, sir, until they find their perfect home," the store owner said with a smile.

The man looked at Molly again, "She is quite pretty and maybe she will be exactly what my daughter needs."

Molly was rushed to the cash register, placed in a gift bag and scooped up.

"I am going to be late," the man said as he looked at his watch.

The store owner waved as the man hurried out of the store and walked briskly down the sidewalk.

It was getting dark now and Molly was getting scared. The man was walking so fast that the bag broke and Molly tumbled to the ground messing up her hair and denting her box. The man snatched her up and kept walking.

As Molly and the man entered the hospital room he said, "Grace are you ready to go home?

"Oh yes Daddy, I am feeling better and can't wait to go home! What's behind your back, Daddy?"

"It is a special gift to cheer you up. Do you want to see what it is?"

"Oh yes please" Grace said smiling.

Molly tried to smile her brightest smile.

As the man pulled her from behind his back the little girl held her arms out wide, "Oh, Daddy, a dolly. A beautiful dolly!"

"Her name is Molly and she is a ballerina," said her father.

"She is perfect," Grace laughed and she took Molly into her arms.

Molly should have been happy, but when the little girl spun her around and Molly could see her, she realized she was in a wheelchair.

"How could we dance?" Molly thought.

Grace carefully placed Molly in her lap and said, "I can't wait to get you to your new home, and I really hope you like it."

Molly's head hung down as she and the girl were wheeled to the car.

On the way home, Molly wondered how this could have happened. After all the time she had waited to be chosen and how she would never dance.

When they got home, Grace said with a smile, "Molly, would you like to see my room?"

Molly tried to smile and held her breath, so as not to cry.

As they entered her room, Molly looked up to see pictures of ballerinas all over the walls, ballet slippers hanging from the bedpost and a beautiful gown hanging in the closet.

The little girl wheeled over to her radio, switched on the music and said, "I will guess you like to dance. I was a dancer too, but I was in an accident. Don't worry though, I have learned to dance without my feet."

With that, Grace gracefully spun around in her wheelchair to the music with Molly. As Molly's hair blew and her dress swayed with each turn, she bagan to smile.

Grace scooped Molly into the air, gave her a big hug and said, "I will take wonderful care of you from now on. We will dance and be the best of friends. I love you already, Molly."

Molly rested her head on Grace's shoulder and thought, "There is a perfect home for everyone, and this one is mine." She hugged Grace gently and whispered, "I love you too."

the end

www.ingramcontent.com/pod-product-compliance
Lightning Source LLC
Chambersburg PA
CBHW041926090426
42743CB00020B/3458